SCIENCE
GETS IT
WRONG

THAT BULL
IS SEEING
RED!

SCIENCE'S BIGGEST MISTAKES ABOUT ANIMALS AND PLANTS

CHRISTINE ZUCHORA-WALSKE

Lerner Publications Company • Minneapolis

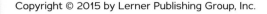

Lerner Publications Company
A division of Lerner Publishing Group, Inc.
241 First Avenue North
Minneapolis, MN 55401 USA

For reading levels and more information, look up this title at www.lernerbooks.com.

Library of Congress Cataloging-in-Publication Data

Zuchora-Walske, Christine, author.
    That bull is seeing red! : science's biggest mistakes about animals and
plants / by Christine Zuchora-Walske.
        pages   cm. — (Science gets it wrong)
    Includes index.
    ISBN 978–1–4677–3660–2 (lib. bdg. : alk. paper)
    ISBN 978–1–4677–4737–0 (eBook)
    1. Animals—Juvenile literature. 2. Plants—Juvenile literature. 3. Errors, Scientific—
Juvenile literature. I. Title.
    QL50 2015
    500—dc23   2013039325

Manufactured in the United States of America
1 — MG — 7/15/14

CONTENTS

Mice can grow from sweaty shirts.
Plants eat soil.
Some plants eat humans!

In earlier times, thousands—maybe millions—of people believed ideas like these. These theories were once examples of the best available scientific thinking.

For as long as humans have existed, we've tried to understand the world in which we live. Early humans used simple methods to examine the animals and plants around them. They asked questions, made observations, and performed tests. These steps became the basis of scientific practice. Over time, people developed new observation tools, such as lenses for magnifying and instruments for measuring.

As scientists improved people's knowledge of the world, sometimes they confirmed old ideas. Sometimes they realized those ideas had been terribly wrong. Oops!

Science is a constant search for new facts. And new facts can reveal problems with old beliefs.

So go ahead and laugh at the silly science of the past. But remember, someday in the future, people might think our scientific ideas are pretty goofy too!

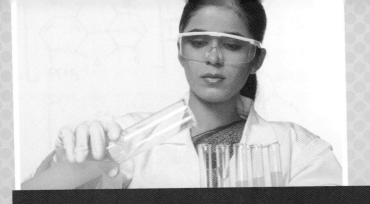

SWEAT + WHEAT = MICE?

Ever found a forgotten sandwich in your backpack? Maybe it started out as PBJ on wheat and turned into fruit flies on mold. Eww.

Since ancient times, people have noticed creepy-crawly living things appearing on nonliving stuff. Some scholars from those times assumed that the crawly things had sprouted from the other matter. This is called **spontaneous generation**.

In ancient China, people thought that aphids grew from bamboo plants. The people of Babylon (in Iraq) believed that mud produced worms. Ancient Greek scholars had similar beliefs. Aristotle (384–322 BCE) suggested that animals can come either from other animals or from "soul-heat." Soul-heat acts on matter to produce living things. Aristotle's theory survived two thousand years.

Then scientists began controlling their experiments more tightly. And they started using microscopes to view organisms that people had never seen before. In 1668, Italian scientist Francesco Redi did an experiment. He thought maggots in rotting meat came from fly eggs laid in the meat, not from the meat itself. (At the time, few people shared this belief.) He placed meat in different containers. Some containers were

spontaneous generation: living things sprouting from nonliving material

open, others were sealed, and others were covered with fabric. As Redi predicted, maggots appeared only in the exposed meat.

HOW TO MAKE MICE

In the 1600s, Belgian scientist Jan Baptist van Helmont wrote a recipe for making mice. You just put a sweaty shirt and some wheat into an open jar. Wait twenty-one days, and—voila!—the wheat changes into mice.

Despite Redi's demonstration, the debate over spontaneous generation continued for two centuries. Arguments turned toward microscopic organisms. Some scientists claimed that even after boiling broth to kill **microbes**, the broth could still spontaneously generate more microbes.

In the late 1800s, a French chemist named Louis Pasteur settled this debate. Pasteur boiled broth in a flask with an S-shaped neck. Air could enter the flask, but microbes from the air settled in the neck. No microbes grew in Pasteur's boiled broth. Yet after he tipped the broth into the neck, it grew cloudy with microbes. This experiment proved that microbes cannot grow from sterile (microbe-free) broth. But they grow from microbes already present in the air.

Louis Pasteur

So don't worry. Your next PBJ won't transform into a flies-and-mold sandwich. Not unless you give your local flies and fungi some time to get cozy in your backpack.

microbes: microscopic organisms

BUMBLEBEES SOAR ABOVE THE LAWS OF NATURE

Look closely at the bumblebees above.
Check out the size of their bodies compared to the size of their teensy wings. A bumblebee looks like a fat, fuzzy bear. How on Earth does it fly?

If you're curious about that, you're not the first. Back in the 1930s, an **entomologist** named August Magnan wondered the same thing.

The first controlled airplane flight had happened in 1903. At that time, scientists studied the science of flight. These studies improved **aviation**. They also brought better understanding of how air and solid objects interact.

In 1934, Magnan published a book titled *La vol des insectes (The Flight of Insects).* In it, he wrote, "Prompted by what is done in aviation, I applied the laws of air resistance to insects, and I arrived, with [my assistant] Mr. Sainte-Laguë, at this conclusion: that their flight is impossible." Magnan argued that the bumblebee's tiny wings shouldn't be able to keep the beefy bug airborne.

Magnan's findings inspired awe about the bumblebee.

aviation: airplane design and operation

entomologist: a scientist who studies insects

Did this creature really soar above the laws of nature? Well, although people in Magnan's time couldn't figure out how bees flew, scientists solved the puzzle soon afterward.

Magnan himself spotted one problem with his calculations. He had assumed that like airplane wings, bees' wings are smooth plates. Then he saw the wings under a microscope. He realized that they weren't smooth and that his math was wrong.

Later, scientists outlined the fine points of bee flight. In 2005, bioengineer Michael Dickinson and his colleagues studied bees in motion using high-speed digital photography. They found that the bee's secret is short, rotating, superfast wing strokes. Bees beat their wings 230 times per second.

According to Dickinson, since modern scientists know exactly how bees fly, you're "no longer allowed to use this story about not understanding bee flight as an example of where science has failed, because it is just not true."

FLYING KITTIES

You've probably heard that cats have nine lives and always land on their feet. Maybe you're tempted to test these ideas. But there's no need! Please, put the kitty down.

Long ago, humans noticed cats' keen senses and nimble bodies. But they still wondered: how do cats survive falls that would injure or kill other creatures?

No one really knew until Étienne-Jules Marey came along. Marey was a French **physiologist**. He recorded the movements of bodies in a series of photographs. He called this practice chronophotography.

Marey wanted to know how a cat lands on its feet. In the 1880s, he photographed falling felines. His photos show exactly how a cat twists its body into landing position. Marey concluded that cats have a unique gift for landing on their feet. Later scientists supported Marey's idea. The gift became known as the righting reflex. When a fall triggers the righting reflex, a cat uses its eyes, its sense of balance, and its flexibility to put its body through a series of twists and leg movements before ending up legs down.

physiologist: a scientist who studies the processes of living bodies

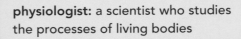

But how often do cats actually survive falls? In 1987, New York City's Animal Medical Center studied 132 cats that had been treated after falls from tall buildings. Ninety percent of these cats survived. However, most had serious injuries. These included bruised and collapsed lungs, broken and dislocated bones, and more. The number of injuries per cat rose with the distance fallen, up to seven stories. But above seven stories, the number of injuries per cat fell sharply. The researchers concluded that given enough time to position themselves, falling cats can limit their injuries.

A decade later, veterinarians at the University of Zagreb in Croatia did a similar study of 119 cats. These researchers got very different results. More than 96 percent of those cats survived. But most of those suffered severe injuries. And falls from the seventh story or higher caused *more* severe injuries. With the righting reflex, cats do have a talent for landing on their feet. But that doesn't mean they get off easy every time—a cat that falls from a great height probably won't walk away unharmed.

SUNFLOWER BLOSSOMS WORSHIP THE SUN

If you've ever taken a road trip through the North American countryside, you've probably seen fields of blooming sunflowers. These flowers are so big and bright that they're hard to miss. That's especially true if they're all pointing in the same direction. Perhaps because of that eye-catching sight—and because sunflower blossoms look like mini suns—people have long believed that sunflower blossoms are **heliotropic**. That means they follow the sun as it moves across the sky.

The sunflower's name has boosted this belief. In fact, the first part of the sunflower's scientific name, *Helianthus,* means "sunlike flower." And in many other languages, the flower's name translates to "turn to the sun."

Those names were given a long time ago. But many modern gardening experts continue to claim that sunflowers are heliotropic. Search for information on sunflowers and heliotropism at the library or online. Even some modern books or articles written by scientists suggest that sunflower blossoms track the sun.

heliotropic: moving to face the sun as it crosses the sky

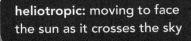

But no matter how many experts say that sunflower blossoms track the sun, it just isn't true. It is true that the flower heads face in the same general direction. But that direction—east—is always constant.

Here's one other reason why myths about sunflowers persist. Young sunflower buds do track the sun. On a sunny day, the buds follow the sun across the sky from east to west. Overnight the buds slowly turn to face east, ready for the next sunrise. But as the flower buds mature and bloom, the stems stiffen. The blossoms are fixed in an east-facing position.

Scientists—some of them, anyway—have known this at least since 1882. In August of that year, members of the Academy of Natural Sciences of Philadelphia (ANSP) discussed sunflower heliotropism. At the time, ANSP was the United States' most respected natural science society. People at the meeting shared observations about sunflower blossoms at different times of the day. These observations show clearly that sunflower blossoms do not follow the sun. They always face east.

So if you're ever lost out on the Great Plains on a cloudy day and you can't tell which direction is which, just look for the nearest sunflower field. It will tell you which way is east. And with several thousand sunflowers per acre, the message will come across loud and clear!

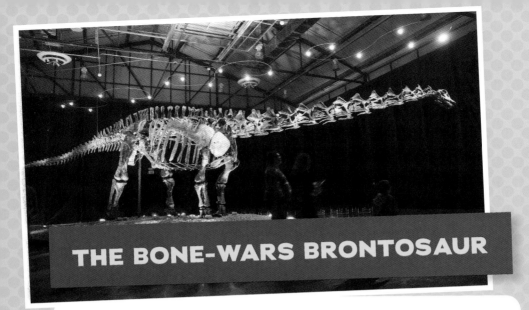

THE BONE-WARS BRONTOSAUR

When you see the word *scientist*, what do you picture? A shy know-it-all who lives at the lab? Some scientists might fit that description. But scientists have all kinds of personalities. And sometimes they make spectacular fools of themselves.

Edward Drinker Cope and Othniel Charles Marsh were rising stars in **paleontology** during the 1870s and the 1880s. Each scientist wanted to discover more **fossils**, name more species, and publish more papers than the other. Cope and Marsh's bitter Bone Wars were the talk of the US scientific community. The Bone Wars even made newspaper headlines.

In their race to claim the best, the biggest, the most, and the most unusual fossils, Cope and Marsh made many mistakes. They wrongly identified some fossils. They hurriedly named others. They wrote papers that introduced those mistakes to other scientists and to the public. Later, paleontologists needed many years to correct these goofs.

paleontology: the study of ancient plant and animal fossils

fossils: preserved remains or traces of ancient living things

One Bone Wars goof had an especially long life. Marsh's assistant sent him a not-quite-complete skeleton of a giant **sauropod** from Wyoming. Marsh declared it was a new species. He

Edward Drinker Cope

called it *Brontosaurus* (thunder lizard). He wanted to display it at the museum he directed in Connecticut. So in 1883, he completed the skeleton with other bones from the same spot in Wyoming. He assumed these bones too were from brontosaurs. Marsh's *Brontosaurus* became a world-famous dinosaur.

There's just one problem. *Brontosaurus* never existed. Most of the skeleton was formed from the bones of a very large *Apatosaurus*—a dinosaur that had been discovered several years earlier. The brontosaur's skull came from a *Camarasaurus*. Other scientists didn't discover this mistake until 1903—years after both Marsh and Cope had died. But the public loved *Brontosaurus* so much that the imaginary dinosaur lived on for decades in books and in museum displays.

Matt Lamanna, curator at the Carnegie Museum of Natural History in Pittsburgh, thinks *Brontosaurus* stuck around so long largely because it had a great name. "Thunder lizard" is dramatic. *Apatosaurus*, on the other hand, means "deceptive lizard." For a thunderous dinosaur, *Brontosaurus* did a sneaky job of grabbing the spotlight!

sauropod: a huge, long-necked, plant-eating dinosaur

Plants grow by eating dirt. That's a scary thought. Think about all the plants that have lived on Earth since life began. Then think about all the dirt those plants would have eaten: a whole lot of it. Would we have any planet left?

Thousands of years ago, scientists in ancient Greece claimed that plants grew this way. Luckily, the Greeks were wrong. They had based their guess on what they could see with the naked eye. The Greeks noticed plants rooted in soil. They watched the plants grow larger. The Greeks knew the plants must have gained matter from somewhere. And the only source they could see was the soil.

The Greek idea held sway until Europe's Renaissance period (1300s–1600s). Then European scholars began to question long-accepted ancient Greek ideas. Until this time, few people had tested these ideas. In 1450, German scholar Nicholas of Cusa suggested an experiment to test his idea that plants consume water, not soil.

Two centuries later, someone finally performed this experiment. In 1648, Jan Baptist van Helmont weighed a pot of soil and then began to grow a willow tree within it. After five years, he found that the willow tree had gained about 163 pounds (74 kilograms). The weight of the soil had hardly changed. So Helmont concluded (wrongly) that the extra matter had come from the water.

In 1771, English scholar Joseph Priestley put a mint plant in a closed container with a burning candle. The candle flame used up the oxygen and went out. But later, Priestley was able to relight the candle. He realized that the plant produced a gas that allowed the flame to burn.

Joseph Priestley

After this discovery, other scientists figured out, little by little, exactly how plants survive and grow. They don't eat soil *or* water. In fact, they don't consume anything that comes from outside their own bodies. Instead, they make their own food.

Plants make their own food by **photosynthesis**. During photosynthesis, plants use energy from the sun to combine carbon dioxide from the air and hydrogen from water to make sugars. This process releases oxygen into the atmosphere. A plant stores some of the sugars it has made. It uses the rest for energy. It's a self-supplying sugar factory!

photosynthesis: a process in which plants use energy from the sun to make sugar for energy and growth

BLIND AS A BAT

If you wear glasses, you might say that you're as blind as a bat without them. The problem is bats aren't blind!

Who came up with the myth of the blind bat? The experts at Bat Conservation International think it started when people realized that bats can find food—and find their way around—even when they can't see.

In earlier times, most people thought that bats were good night fliers because they had unusually keen eyesight. But an Italian scientist named Lazzaro Spallanzani wondered whether bats could even see in the dark. In 1793, Spallanzani performed a series of experiments with bats. He blinded a bat by removing its eyeballs. The bat flew skillfully around its cave anyway.

Spallanzani performed many more experiments after that. He kept getting similar results. He also found that blinded bats could still hunt insects. He concluded that a bat's eyes must be unimportant for flying and hunting.

In this case, science didn't get it wrong—but people likely got the wrong impression from science. Some people who heard about Spallanzani's work probably misunderstood it. They may have thought that *unimportant* meant useless. The popular wisdom about bats began to change. People began saying that bats are blind.

Lazzaro Spallanzani *(right)*

Many bats have small eyes hidden by thick fur. This may have led even more people to believe that the animals can't see very well. But that couldn't be

ECHOLOCATION

To find their way in the dark, most bats use echolocation. They make high-pitched sounds. Then they listen as the echoes of those sounds bounce off objects in their path. Bats' brains make visual maps from the information the echoes provide.

further from the truth. Bats can see just fine. And many bats see better than people do. The big fruit bats of Asia, Africa, and Australia have large eyes and excellent eyesight. They use their eyes to find their favorite foods in the dark of night.

It's true that small, insect-eating bats mainly use sound to direct themselves and hunt. But even these bats use their sight. Bat scientist Paul Faure explains, "All bats can see and all bats are sensitive to changing light levels because this is the main cue that they use to sense when it is . . . time to become active." So if you must compare your terrible eyesight to an animal's, try a mole instead. It *is* nearly blind!

Pitcher plant

BEWARE THE CANNIBAL TREE!

"The atrocious cannibal tree . . . came to sudden, savage life. . . . The tendrils . . . like great green serpents . . . rose . . . and wrapped her about . . . with the cruel swiftness . . . of anacondas fastening upon their prey."

In colorful, creepy detail, a scientist named Karl Leche described a scene he had witnessed in Madagascar. Leche wrote about the "cannibal tree" in a letter to his friend and fellow scientist, Omelius Friedlowsky. Friedlowsky shared the story with the *New York World* newspaper.

Published in 1874, the story spread like wildfire. Other newspapers and magazines around the world ran with Leche's tale. Before long, almost everyone knew about the man-eating tree of Madagascar. Leche had given it the scientific name *Crinoida dajeeana*. And because the story was published as nonfiction, many people believed the account.

Why were people so easily convinced? About one century earlier, European scientists had discovered certain plants, such as the Venus flytrap, that ate animals. The news had shocked the public. Animals were supposed to eat plants, not the other way around! But once more people saw these plants for themselves, it must have seemed perfectly logical that some of them might devour humans.

The idea of human-eating plants got a boost in 1924. That year, a travel writer published a book titled *Madagascar, Land of the Man-Eating Tree.* The author was Chase Osborn, a former governor of Michigan. Osborn already had people's trust due to his political position. And he claimed that many residents of Madagascar had confirmed the tree's existence.

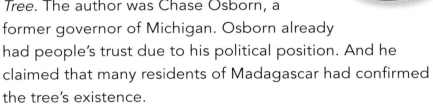

Chase Osborn

The scientific community didn't prove that the man-eating tree was imaginary until 1955. Science writer Willy Ley figured out that the writer Edmund Spencer had invented Karl Leche, Omelius Friedlowsky, and their entire story. Madagascar's only **carnivorous** plant is a pitcher plant not quite big enough to eat a mouse.

A rat is the largest animal known to have been eaten by a carnivorous plant. It's the favorite meal of a giant pitcher plant called *Nepenthes attenboroughii.* It lures rats with a pitcher-shaped flower full of sweet sap. When a rat leans in to drink the sap, it slips on the pitcher's waxy inner surface. Then it gets stuck in the gooey sap. Digestive enzymes (like the acid in your stomach) then break down the live rat.

It's a horrible way to go, for sure. Thank goodness no pitcher plants are anywhere near big enough to trap a person!

carnivorous: meat eating

DON'T JUMP, LITTLE LEMMINGS!

Dozens of fat, furry lemmings scamper across the movie screen. Then a narrator declares, "A kind of [urge] seizes each tiny rodent and . . . each falls into step for a march that will take them to a strange destiny." The lemmings stream toward a cliff on the Arctic Ocean. When they reach the edge, "over they go, casting themselves into the sea."

Lemmings are small rodents that live on the Arctic tundra, a treeless plain surrounding the North Pole. The bizarre scene occurs in Walt Disney Productions' 1958 nature documentary *White Wilderness.* It promotes the idea that every few years, lemmings commit mass suicide. *White Wilderness* won the 1958 Academy Award for Best Documentary Feature. So the lemming bit must be true, right?

Wrong. The whole scene was faked! But the film's director, James Algar, didn't invent the idea. The concept of suicidal lemmings had been around for a long time.

For centuries—at least since the 1500s—people had noticed that every three or four years, lemming populations

exploded and then rapidly shrank. They saw live lemmings on the move and dead lemmings in the water. They concluded that when lemmings grew too numerous, many lemmings would kill themselves. This suicide would protect the species from starvation and disease.

Thanks to a 1980s investigation by journalist Brian Vallee, we know the truth about the lemming

FILM FAKERY

James Algar *(center)* filmed *White Wilderness* in Alberta, Canada. Alberta does not border the Arctic Ocean. No lemmings live in the filming area. So the film's crew brought lemmings from hundreds of miles away. They filmed the lemmings running on a snow-covered turntable. Then they herded the lemmings over a small cliff into a river. They made the setting look realistic with tight close-ups and many different camera angles.

scene in *White Wilderness.* And biologists have smashed the notion that lemmings commit suicide.

Here's what really happens. Lemmings eat grass, berries, bark, leaves, roots, and moss. When they've eaten up the local food supply, they travel in large numbers to search for food. Many of them die during the trip. They can swim, but they're not great at it. When they come to a body of water, they try to cross it. Sometimes they drown. "If they get wet to the skin," says zoologist Gordon Jarrell, "they're essentially dead."

Have you ever heard a parent say that he or she is seeing red? Maybe your baby sister just flung her mashed carrots at the wall . . . for the third time. Or your dog tracked mud through the house. Bottom line, your parent is ticked off.

Seeing red means "being downright angry." If you're seeing red, you're about to lose your temper. This saying comes from the idea that the color red enrages bulls. And that idea developed following observations of bulls during bullfighting. People drew from their observations what seemed to be a logical conclusion. Seems like a scientific approach, right? But they didn't realize they had considered only one possibility out of many.

Bullfighting is a form of entertainment popular in Spain, Portugal, and Latin America. In a bullfight, a performer called a matador taunts a bull. The matador whips around a special cape to anger the bull and make it charge. The cape is often red. Sometimes it's magenta and gold. The matador tries to draw the bull as near as possible without suffering an injury.

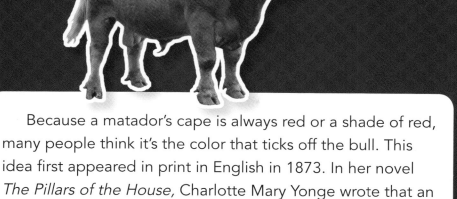

Because a matador's cape is always red or a shade of red, many people think it's the color that ticks off the bull. This idea first appeared in print in English in 1873. In her novel *The Pillars of the House,* Charlotte Mary Yonge wrote that an offensive remark "is like a red rag to a bull."

But the truth is bulls don't even see red. Their vision is **dichromatic**. That means they can distinguish only two of the three primary colors. They can tell yellow and blue but red . . . not so much. It's the movement of the cape that really makes bulls charge.

Cattle see flapping as a sign of danger. In everyday situations, cattle back away from flapping objects or simply refuse to move. But a bullfighting ring is not a normal environment. The bull can't find a corner to retreat to nor an opening to escape through. So it defends itself by attacking the flapping object.

The idea that red enrages bulls, it turns out, is just a bunch of bull.

dichromatic: able to tell apart only two of the three primary colors (red, yellow, and blue)

Eyebright

PLANT-VERTISING

Are your eyes bloodshot? You need some eyebright. The petals of the eyebright flower are striped, like the lines across bloodshot eyes. Do you have a headache? Try a dose of walnuts! Walnuts look just like brains. It's obvious. Plants that look like your ailing body parts provide the cures you need.

For many centuries, that's what some healers believed. The earliest record of this idea came from ancient Greece. In *Natural History* (65 CE), the Greek scholar Pliny wrote, "The Herb Scorpius resembles the tail of the Scorpion, and is good against [a scorpion's] biting."

Healers practiced this idea in many forms for centuries. In the first half of the 1500s, a German-Swiss doctor named Paracelsus expanded on the idea. He declared that "nature marks each growth . . . according to its curative benefit." In other words: the shape, the color, the taste, the smell, or another trait of a plant suggests its usefulness in healing.

This idea became known as the **doctrine** of signatures. *Signatures* meant "physical signs of healing power." Medical books included the doctrine through the 1800s.

doctrine: rule

Before the 1800s ended, however, some scientists began to question this belief. They started testing plant-based medicines more carefully. Through testing, the scientists discovered which plants were more likely to heal which ailments. They found that plants with signatures seldom led to healing.

The next time you get a headache, you could take the advice of seventeenth-century botanist William Coles. Crush a walnut, moisten it, and place the soggy blob on the crown of your head. This, he promises, "comforts the brain and head mightily." Or you could ask an adult for some ibuprofen, drink a glass of water, and take a nap. Which one do you think will work better?

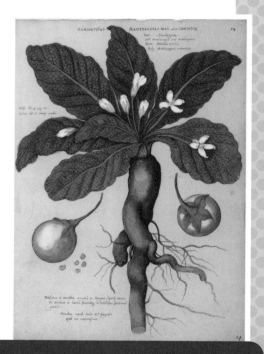

THE MAGICAL MANDRAKE

The mandrake is a plant with a thick, fleshy root. The root often looks like a human body. According to the doctrine of signatures, the mandrake helps women become pregnant. All they need to do is place mandrakes under their pillows. But they'd better be careful. A superstition of earlier times warned that harvesting mandrakes is dangerous business. Demons live in mandrake roots, and they give a fatal shriek when pulled from the ground!

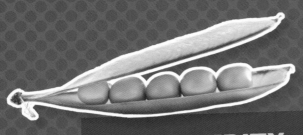

HEREDITY: LIKE MIXING PAINT

Heredity is the passing of traits from parents to offspring. And before the mid-1800s, no one had a clue how it worked.

Sure, people noticed patterns. They saw that plants and animals passed certain traits on to their young. And farmers had successfully reproduced favorable traits while breeding animals and plants. But people couldn't figure out why one offspring of a pairing resembled its mother while another offspring resembled its father.

The Greek scholar Aristotle believed that particles called pangenes came together from all parts of the body to form eggs and sperm used in reproduction. His theory lasted from the 300s BCE to the 1800s. In the 1600s, two scientists developed competing ideas. Dutch scientist Anton van Leeuwenhoek proposed that all inherited traits come from the father. Dutch doctor Regnier de Graaf argued that all inherited traits come from the mother.

In the early 1800s, the blending theory of heredity grew popular. This theory said that parents' traits blend like paint to form the traits of the offspring. So a blue parakeet mating with a yellow parakeet would have a green baby parakeet.

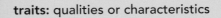

traits: qualities or characteristics

A tall parent and a short parent would have offspring of medium height. But the blending theory couldn't explain how two brown-eyed parents could have a blue-eyed baby.

In 1865, an Austrian scientist named Gregor Mendel started some breeding experiments with pea plants. For instance, Mendel bred a plant with round peas and a plant with wrinkled peas. All the offspring had round peas. When Mendel bred two of the offspring, one-quarter of *their* offspring had wrinkled peas. Mendel concluded that the factors that cause different traits, such as roundness and wrinkledness, occur in paired units. One unit is "dominant." The other type is "recessive." A dominant unit hides the recessive unit with which it is paired.

Gregor Mendel

Later, scientists found that not all organisms pass on their genes in the same way as the pea plant. But many organisms do show similar inheritance patterns. Modern scientists still use Mendel's principles to explain the basic rules of heredity.

It turns out that heredity is more like shuffling a deck of cards than mixing paint. Scientists continue to learn how the different "cards"—or genes—interact with one another. As they do, the game of heredity makes more sense to everyone.

SOURCE NOTES

8 "Hovering Is a Bother for Bees: Fast Flight Is More Stable," *ScienceDaily,* March 14, 2013, http://www.sciencedaily.com /releases/2013/03/130314110609.htm.

9 Kathy Svitil, "Deciphering the Mystery of Bee Flight," California Institute of Technology, November 29, 2005, http://www.caltech.edu/content /deciphering-mystery-bee-flight.

12 Cindy Haynes and Ann Marie VanDerZanden, "Sunflowers," *Iowa State University Extension and Outreach: Horticulture and Home Pest News,* July 27, 2005, http://www.ipm.iastate.edu/ipm/hortnews/node/43.

12 Kate Weinberg, "How to Grow: Sunflowers," *Telegraph* (London), June 6, 2013, http://www.telegraph.co.uk/gardening/howtogrow/5540994 /How-to-grow-sunflowers.html.

19 Cristen Conger, "Are Bats Blind?," *Discovery News,* May 13, 2010, http:// news.discovery.com/earth/are-bats-blind.htm.

20 Edmund Spencer, "Wonderful Stories—The Man-Eating Tree," *Current Literature,* August 1888, accessed September 22, 2013, http://books .google.com/books?id=T_ZYAAAAYAAJ&printsec=frontcover#v= onepage&q&f=false.

20 Ibid.

22 Riley Woodford, "Lemming Suicide Myth: Disney Film Faked Bogus Behavior," Alaska Department of Fish and Game, accessed September 23, 2013, http://www.adfg.alaska.gov/index.cfm?adfg=wildlifenews.view_ article&articles_id=56.

23 Ibid.

25 Gary Martin, "The Meaning and Origin of the Phrase: See Red," *The Phrase Finder,* accessed September 23, 2013. http://www.phrases.org.uk /meanings/see-red.html.

26 "Paracelsus," *Encyclopædia Britannica Online,* accessed September 24, 2013, http://www.britannica.com/print/topic/442424.

27 Ibid.

LERNER

SOURCE

Expand learning beyond the printed book. Download free, complementary educational resources for this book from our website, www.lerneresource.com.

FURTHER INFORMATION

Discovery Kids: Animal Myths
http://kids.discovery.com/tell-me/mythbusters/animal-myths
Are elephants really afraid of mice? Can old dogs learn new tricks? At this Discovery Channel website, you can find answers to popular questions about animals.

Everyday Mysteries: Fun Science Facts from the Library of Congress
http://www.loc.gov/rr/scitech/mysteries/archive.html
This site from the Library of Congress answers common questions about strange topics in fields such as zoology (the study of animals), botany (the study of plant life), chemistry, and more.

Johnson, Jinny. *Animal Planet™ Atlas of Animals.* Minneapolis: Millbrook Press, 2012.
Take in a spectacular view of Earth's wildlife through this book's colorful maps, fascinating facts, and stunning photos.

—*Animal Planet™ Wild World: An Encyclopedia of Animals.* Minneapolis: Millbrook Press, 2012.
Explore the animal world, from the smallest insects to the largest mammal, with this wide-reaching book.

Krieger, Emily. *Myths Busted! Just When You Thought You Knew What You Knew.* Washington, DC: National Geographic, 2013.
You can't believe everything you're told. Check out this book's interesting tidbits and "unthink" facts you've taken as the truth.

Margles, Samantha. *Mythbusters Science Fair Book.* New York: Scholastic, 2011.
This book is packed with dozens of myth-busting science fair projects you can do at school or at home.

National Wildlife Federation: The Truth about Animal Clichés
http://www.nwf.org/News-and-Magazines/National-Wildlife/Animals /Archives/2003/American-Heritage-Animal-Cliches.aspx
This site takes a look at some familiar sayings about animals, such as "quiet as a mouse" and "eats like a bird," and explains whether there's truth behind the clichés.

Silverman, Buffy. *Can an Old Dog Learn New Tricks? And Other Questions about Animals.* Minneapolis: Lerner Publications, 2010.
This book helps readers investigate seventeen statements about animals. Find out which ones are right, which ones are wrong, and which ones still stump scientists.

Strange Science
http://science.discovery.com/strange-science
At this site by the Science Channel, you can explore science hoaxes, science feuds, science mistakes, and more.

INDEX

PHOTO ACKNOWLEDGMENTS

The images in this book are used with the permission of: © iStockphoto.com/
Antagain, pp. 2, 8 (right); 9 (bottom right); © iStockphoto.com/CamiloTorres,
pp. 3 (bottom), 6 (bottom); © iStockphoto.com/vnlit, pp. 3 (top), 8 (left), 9 (top,
bottom left); © iStockphoto.com/yenwen, p. 4; © iStockphoto.com/alptraum,
pp. 5 (top), 7 (bottom); © Sergey Skleznev/Dreamstime.com, p. 5 (bottom);
© photosindia/Getty Images, p. 6 (top); Courtesy of the National Library of
Medicine, pp. 7 (top), 17, 29 (bottom); U.S. Navy/Wikimedia Commons, p. 9
(bottom center); © Jane Burton/Dorling Kindersley/Getty Images, pp. 10, 11
(top); © iStockphoto.com/prill, p. 11 (bottom); © iStockphoto.com/akiyoko,
p. 12 (top); © Pangfolio/Dreamstime.com, pp. 12 (bottom), 13; TOMAS BRAVO/
REUTERS/Newscom, p. 14; Frederick Gutekunst/Wikimedia Commons, p. 15;
© Bogdan Wańkowicz/Dreamstime.com, p. 16; © iStockphoto.com/CraigRJD,
pp. 18, 19 (bottom); © Universal Images Group/SuperStock, p. 19 (top);
© Minden Pictures/SuperStock, p. 20; Library of Congress (LC-DIG-hec-17971),
p. 21; © Sven-Erik Arndt/Picture Press/Getty Images, p. 22 (top); © Juniors/
SuperStock, pp. 22 (bottom), 23 (bottom); Everett Collection, p. 23 (top);
© Natursports/Dreamstime.com, p. 24; © Valenta/Shutterstock.com, p. 25 (top);
© iStockphoto.com/GlobalP, p. 25 (bottom); © Rbiedermann/Dreamstime.com,
pp. 26; p. 27 (bottom); © Science Source, p. 27 (top); © iStockphoto.com/Smitt,
pp. 28; 29 (top).

Front cover: © efecreata photography/Shutterstock.com (top); © Roberto Cerruti/
Shutterstock.com (bottom).